BAIT AND SWITCH

by Richard Dresser

S A M U E L   F R E N C H ,   I N C .
45 West 25th Street   NEW YORK 10010
7623 Sunset Boulevard   HOLLYWOOD 90046
LONDON   *TORONTO*

IMPORTANT BILLING AND CREDIT REQUIREMENTS

All producers of BAIT AND SWITCH *must* give credit to the Author of the Play in all programs distributed in connection with performances of the Play and in all instances in which the title of the Play appears for purposes of advertising, publicizing or otherwise exploiting the Play and/or a production. The name of the Author *must* also appear on a separate line, on which no other name appears, immediately following the title, and *must* appear in size of type not less than fifty percent the size of the title type.

Bait and Switch was developed in a longer form at New Dramatists with John Pynchon Holms and Lynn Holst dramaturgs, and later at the Eugene O'Neill National Playwrights Conference, with Barnet Kellman directing and Max Wilk dramaturg.

The play was first presented in New York in January of 1990 at the West Bank Cafe's Downstairs Theater Bar, Lewis Black, Rand Foerster, and Rusty Magee Artistic Directors. *Bait and Switch* was directed by John Pynchon Holms with the following cast:

GARY	Donald Berman
DOUG	Doug Ballard
LUCY	Cynthia Carle
KENNY	Larry Pine
ERICA	Ritamarie Kelly

(The role of GARY was later played by James Gleason.)

CHARACTERS

GARY
DOUG, his older brother
LUCY, his wife
KENNY, a lawyer
ERIC, a waitress

TIME

End of the summer.

PLACE

The Beachside Bar & Grill, on a boardwalk on
the New Jersey shore.

(The Sinatra song "That's Life." Then LIGHTS up on the Beachside Bar & Grill, on a boardwalk on the New Jersey shore. There's a bar to one side, a jukebox, and tables with red and white checked tablecloths. GARY is sitting by himself, wearing a suit and drinking a glass of milk. His briefcase is on the floor. DOUG enters. He's older than Gary and casually dressed. HE comes over and stares at Gary. The song ends.)*

DOUG. You going to church, Gary? Huh?

GARY. I'm not going to church.

DOUG. You sure look like you're going to church, dressed up like that. He's our buddy, we're having a drink with our buddy. You gotta relax.

GARY. I'm relaxed, okay?

DOUG. *(Re: glass of milk.)* What the fuck is that?

GARY. That's milk. It comes from cows.

DOUG. You better lose it before he gets here.

GARY. Doug, my stomach is killing me. I get these pains—

DOUG. Your stomach. Your fucking stomach. Don't embarrass me, Gary. *(DOUG sits down.)* You nervous? Is that the problem?

GARY. I guess, I mean this whole thing—

DOUG. You said you were relaxed. Now you're nervous. Am I making you nervous?

GARY. No, Doug. You're not making me nervous.

DOUG. I could do this myself, Gary. You don't have to be here. You could be watching television with your glass

---

*Mention is made of songs which *are* not in the public domain. Producers of this play are hereby cautioned that permission to produce this play does not include rights to use these songs in production. Producers should contact the copyright owners directly for rights.

of milk, how does that sound?

GARY. I'm your partner, Doug. I gotta be here.

(LUCY enters from the kitchen.)

DOUG. Hey, Lucy.

LUCY. Oh, hi, Doug.

DOUG. Would you get me a Jack Daniels? Bring Gary a Chivas.

LUCY. Gary can't drink. He's pre-ulcerous.

DOUG. Get the boy a drink, Lucy. Make it a Chivas and Maalox, okay? *(To Gary.)* You sit here drinking milk, what's he gonna think?

LUCY. Gary? Is that what you want?

GARY. Yeah, that sounds fine, Lucy.

LUCY. 'Member the last time you went drinking?

DOUG. This isn't going drinking. It's having a drink. Maybe it'll calm him down.

(LUCY goes to make the drinks.)

GARY. I'm calm, for Chrissakes. What makes me upset right now is you saying I'm not calm.

DOUG. Okay, you're calm, just make sure you stay that way. I need you on my side today.

GARY. This is a sure thing, right? He's definitely in?

DOUG. Absolutely. Absolutely. We shmooze him a little, da-dip, da-dip da-doo and we're outta the woods.

GARY. I really want to thank you, Doug. It's been a bitch of a summer trying to get this thing on its feet.

DOUG. Lighten up, Gary. You're too fucking serious. That's why your stomach is screwed up. You gotta learn to express your feelings, not keep 'em all bottled up inside—

(LUCY puts the drinks on the table.)

DOUG. Lucy, would you set these tables up like people might be coming? I want the place to look decent for him.

LUCY. We'd need a coupla bulldozers to make this place look decent.

GARY. *(To Lucy.)* Doug says it's a sure thing with this guy.

LUCY. Doug said the restaurant was a sure thing, too. That's why you put your money in it.

DOUG. It *was* a sure thing! It was a sure thing right up 'til the time it screwed up!

LUCY. How can a sure thing screw up?

DOUG. Open your eyes, sweetie! You know what the problem is.

LUCY. The problem is you two are the only regular customers we get and you own the goddam place.

DOUG. That isn't the problem. Gary, tell her what the problem is.

GARY. Well, it takes time to get established in this business—

DOUG. The problem is the jellyfish! No one comes to the beach with the jellyfish out there! Once the jellyfish take off, the people come back to this beach and we're in business.

GARY. For sure?

DOUG. Yeah, for sure. They come to the beach they come in here. It is an unalterable fact of life as we know it. I maintain buying this place was the smartest thing we ever did.

LUCY. I agree. Just look at the other things you've done.

DOUG. (*To Lucy.*) From you I get total support today or we are truly in deep shit. Am I understood by all parties?

LUCY. So how come you need another partner if this place is still gonna work out?

DOUG. Because of the cash flow situation. Gary, would you tell her to butt out of our business?

GARY. Doug has this thing under control, hon.

LUCY. We never shoulda bought into this place. You know that, don't you, Gary?

DOUG. You want your money back, is that it?

LUCY. That's exactly it.

DOUG. (*Gets out checkbook.*) Here, I'll write you a check, how's that? How much you put in, Gary?

GARY. Wait a second—

DOUG. I'll buy out your share. Next summer when this place is hopping, maybe I'll hire you to wash dishes—

GARY. I want to keep my share. This guy is just coming in to get us over the hump, right? It's still our place.

DOUG. That's right.

GARY. So I'm still in.

LUCY. You're making a big mistake, Gary. You oughta get out while the getting's good.

DOUG. That's the spirit, Gary. Hang tough. (*To Lucy.*) When this guy shows, we're on best behavior, Lucy. Get him the linguini, show him what a classy joint we got.

LUCY. Yeah, this place is nothing but class. (*LUCY goes to the kitchen.*)

GARY. She gets nervous. The kid needs braces, the

shocks are gone on the car, it's one thing after another.

DOUG. You got money to pay for that stuff.

GARY. Doug? I put the whole nut into this place.

DOUG. That's all your money? You never told me you were putting in all your money.

GARY. I wanted to be partners. I wanted to pull my weight.

DOUG. She let you do it?

GARY. She doesn't know. Remember how it was this summer, we kept needing more cash and I kept writing the checks. How could I tell her? Once we get a third partner in here we'll start getting something back. Right?

DOUG. Absolutely. Absolutely.

GARY. I'm just real glad you found someone. I mean I am flat out broke, so this deal is coming at a really perfect time for me. In terms of providing for my loved ones and making a future that is not like a black hole—

DOUG. Yeah, I know, Gary. Now would you try to shut up for a little while? I have to get my mind in order.

GARY. Sure, Doug. No problem.

(GARY and DOUG sit at the table in silence. Then KENNY enters, wearing an expensive suit and carrying a briefcase.)

DOUG. Kenny! Jesus Christ, you look good, Kenny. Doesn't Kenny look good?

GARY. Yeah, you look good, Kenny.

DOUG. Kenny, this here is my little brother, Gary. My partner in this thing.

KENNY. Hi, Gary.

GARY. Hi.

(DOUG pulls up a chair for KENNY, who sits down.)

DOUG. What do you think, pretty nice place, right?

KENNY. Who do you have to screw to get a drink around here?

DOUG. (*Calling out.*) Hey! Lucy!

KENNY. You have to screw Lucy to get a drink?

DOUG. Jeez, you look terrific.

KENNY. You told me that already.

(LUCY enters.)

DOUG. Listen, babe, get my friend here the linguini, and . . .

KENNY. Make it a scotch, would you?

DOUG. Yeah, scotch. Great.

(LUCY exits.)

KENNY. So, you wanna go to bed with me tonight, Dougie?

DOUG. What? What are you saying?

KENNY. I mean, hey, you tell me how nice I look, you order my food for me like I'm a broad—what am I s'posed to think?

DOUG. That's good, Kenny. Like we're on a date. The thing is, I just want you to try the linguini. It's the house specialty.

KENNY. She cook it?

DOUG. Nah, we got a chef, Mike. Super kid, the kind of kid you say, yeah, I wish he was my son.

GARY. He's a really great kid. Just like family.

KENNY. I wouldn't mind taking a shot at her.

DOUG. Lucy?

KENNY. Yeah, I kinda like her. She loses a little weight—

DOUG. We got a good solid staff here. Gary's the day to day manager, I handle the financial side of things—

KENNY. Maybe she doesn't even have to lose the weight. She's the type, you have a coupla drinks and she looks like a million bucks—

GARY. So what's the deal?

KENNY. What?

GARY. What's the deal you got for us?

DOUG. You gotta excuse my brother. He gets a little eager sometimes. The thing is, me and Gary aren't sure we even want a partner—

KENNY. Then why the fuck did you call me?

DOUG. I mean we'll consider it. If the deal is good.

KENNY. You'll consider it, huh?

GARY. We're actually real interested.

KENNY. You guys oughta talk to each other more often. Pull in the same direction, it makes life easy.

DOUG. We talk all the time. We're impressed by your people and if we go the partner route then you're at the top of the list. That's what Gary and I are saying.

KENNY. You're full of shit, Doug. Gary here is telling the truth. This little hole in the wall is dead in the water and you need help—

DOUG. True, we got a bum deal from the jellyfish—

KENNY. What are you talking about? Who are the jellyfish?

DOUG. You know, in the water, those ugly suckers—

KENNY. Oh, jellyfish. Yeah? They're giving you a rough deal?

GARY. The thing is, they bite. People stay away. It hurts business.

KENNY. Tell you what, I'll have my people talk to 'em. They'll leave. How about that, Gary? You like the sound of that? We threaten 'em?

GARY. Sounds great.

DOUG. He's kidding, Gary. How the fuck is he gonna talk to the jellyfish?

GARY. I knew he was kidding.

KENNY. Yeah? You don't know my people.

(LUCY enters with Kenny's scotch. As SHE puts the drink down, HE puts his hand on hers.)

KENNY. You're the prettiest girl I've seen in a long time.

LUCY. You oughta get out more often. (*SHE exits.*)

KENNY. Spunky little number, isn't she? I like 'em like that. They put up a fight but once you get 'em going it's like a runaway train. Where's the bathroom?

DOUG. It's through there on the left.

(KENNY exits.)

DOUG. What the fuck are you doing?

GARY. What are *you* doing? You're telling him we don't want the deal—

DOUG. You string 'em along, Gary, that's the game. Christ!

GARY. He hits on Lucy again, I swear . . .

DOUG. What? What are you gonna do?

GARY. Nobody talks about my wife like that, Doug. Not while I'm sitting here.

DOUG. You wanna lose the deal, Gary?

GARY. I'm counting on the deal.

DOUG. Sounds to me like you lose the deal and you won't even *have* a wife. So try to exercise just a little fucking self-control, would you?

GARY. I've gotta at least tell him she's my wife—

DOUG. Leave that up to me. This thing is a delicate operation. It's like we got Kenny cut open and we're putting in a new heart. I got the scalpel in one hand and Kenny's new heart in the other and you're choosing that exact moment to get on my case with a lot of bullshit. Do you know what I'm saying, Gary?

GARY. I guess you're telling me to shut up again.

(KENNY comes back.)

DOUG. I bet you're thinking how nice it'd be to run a joint like this. Bring your friends in—

KENNY. The bathroom is disgusting.

DOUG. What are you talking about? We keep the place clean. That kinda stuff goes a long way with customers—

KENNY. Looks like one of your customers took up residence there. It's disgusting.

DOUG. What do you mean? How is it disgusting?

KENNY. I'm not gonna tell you *how* it's disgusting. I don't wanna talk about it.

DOUG. Are you implying that our place isn't clean?

KENNY. Go check it, Doug.

DOUG. This is impossible. Gary, talk to Kenny while

I'm gone. (*DOUG leaves.*)

GARY. So, you represent other people on this deal?

KENNY. He didn't tell you who my people are?

GARY. Well, he just said they were people—

KENNY. They are very big people—

GARY. Like anyone I would know?

KENNY. Like fucking giants. Very, very big people.

GARY. But Doug and I would continue to actually run the place. I mean we had this plan of running a place since we were kids. My brother and I are a great team together—

KENNY. Nah. If we come in it's ours. Don't kid yourself, Gary.

GARY. Doug didn't explain it that way. He said you were just money people.

KENNY. Doug didn't explain too much, did he?

GARY. Oh, sure he did. We talk all the time.

KENNY. You got another job, Gary?

GARY. Not at the exact present time. I'm too busy running this place—

KENNY. (*Looks around the empty room.*) Must keep you jumping. Anyone ever come in here?

GARY. You gotta understand, this is a slow night in the business.

KENNY. Of course, Friday night, that's always a slow night for restaurants.

GARY. Yeah, well, when the jellyfish aren't out there—

KENNY. You guys with your fucking jellyfish. Honest to God.

(*LUCY enters with the linguini.*)

KENNY. Thanks, doll. You like working here?

LUCY. It's okay.

KENNY. You want to stay on after we buy?

LUCY. Maybe.

KENNY. I'm the guy to see. I bet we could work something out, you and me.

LUCY. I doubt it.

KENNY. Playing hard to get, huh?

LUCY. We oughta be a perfect match. I'm hard to get and you're hard to take.

KENNY. *(To Gary.)* You see that? She likes me.

(DOUG comes back.)

GARY. How was the bathroom, Doug?

DOUG. This is terrific. This is really fabulous. Mike has the whole week to O.D. and he picks today.

KENNY. Is this the kid you want to adopt?

LUCY. He's not always like this.

GARY. Usually, he can handle it pretty good.

DOUG. He's a fucking genius with pasta but he shoots dope. What are you gonna do? How is that, anyway? Isn't this the best linguini you ever had in your mouth?

KENNY. Did he cook it?

DOUG. What do you mean?

KENNY. I mean did this O.D. guy in the bathroom cook my dinner? That's a pretty fucking simple question, isn't it?

LUCY. I cooked it.

KENNY. I can't eat it.

LUCY. What's wrong with it?

KENNY. Don't take it personally, I just don't want it.

LUCY. I just told you I cooked it. It's as good as Mike's—

DOUG. See? It's the best on the boardwalk—

KENNY. I find the linguini depressing, okay? It's bringing me down. (*HE pushes the plate away.*)

DOUG. Get Kenny another drink.

KENNY. I don't want a drink.

DOUG. He wants a drink.

KENNY. I'll tell you what I want. I want a look at the kitchen.

DOUG. Fair enough, you want to see where your money's going. Come on, the grand tour—

KENNY. I want Lucy to show me. She knows the kitchen, she can show me.

GARY. I could show you the kitchen.

KENNY. Is your name Lucy? (*To Lucy.*) Well? You got time to show me the place?

LUCY. That's up to the manager. Gary, you want me to show Mr. Big the kitchen?

DOUG. Yeah, go ahead—

LUCY. Gary?

GARY. Yeah, okay. Just make it quick.

LUCY. I'll remember this, Gary.

(*KENNY follows LUCY to the kitchen. HE turns to Doug and Gary and punches the air with his fist.*)

DOUG. (*Pushing the plate toward Gary.*) So . . . you want this? He didn't touch it.

GARY. Sometimes you make me sick, Doug.

DOUG. You just don't understand the world of commerce. All these years you want to be my partner in this, my partner in that. I finally bring my kid brother on board and he wimps out.

GARY. I'm not wimping out. I just don't like the thought of, you know, a guy like Kenny coming on to Lucy. Business or no business.

DOUG. Lucy's a big girl. She can take care of herself. Hell, she could be the key to the whole deal. (*HE picks at the linguini.*) Mike's linguini is definitely better. No wonder Kenny didn't like it.

GARY. I got a life insurance policy. It'll keep Lucy going a year anyway. Maybe you can help out after that, just 'til she gets her feet on the ground.

DOUG. Don't talk this way, Gary. It makes me lose my appetite. And I definitely need my appetite if I'm gonna eat this shit.

GARY. I'm just saying if the deal doesn't go down like we hope. I have to consider every option, which is not a lot at this point, seeing as how I have no job and no money and a stack of bills.

DOUG. If you're gonna wallow in all this negative bullshit then I'm gonna have to ask you to leave. (*DOUG pushes the linguini aside and lights a cigarette.*)

GARY. You're gonna ask me to leave my restaurant. I been in here all summer sweating like a monkey while you're off working a straight job. And now you are asking me to leave while Lucy is in the kitchen with a lawyer.

DOUG. All I'm saying is I can close this myself.

GARY. Tell me straight, what happens if he doesn't come in with us?

DOUG. The key is to think positive, Gary. That is one of the biggest keys to my own personal success. I think positive, and I always have money, you ever notice that?

GARY. I'm saying *if* he doesn't. If. I think the time has come to be straight with each other, Doug.

DOUG. If, and it is a very big if, if the deal doesn't go down, then we go belly-up. In straight legal terminology, as I understand it, we are fucked. (*DOUG puts his cigarette out in the linguini.*)

GARY. That bad?

DOUG. But that's not gonna happen. Because I am a surgeon when it comes to deals. This is a man who is eating out of my back pocket and he doesn't know it—

KENNY. (*Enters from kitchen.*) You guys trying to make a fool outta me? Huh?

DOUG. What's wrong? Now you don't like our kitchen?

KENNY. How come you didn't tell me she's married? She's worse than just married, she's happily married. I thought that shit went out with the fifties.

GARY. She told you that?

KENNY. Lady's got class. I don't know what she's doing here.

GARY. She said she's happily married? That's great—

KENNY. So hands off. I respect the institution of marriage as I respect little else in this world. A woman's happily married, I stay away. If they're lonely and desperate and hanging by a thread, that's when I make my move. I won't even touch my wife, 'cause she's happily married.

GARY. I agree, Kenny. If they're happily married leave 'em be.

(*KENNY is eating the linguini.*)

DOUG. Kenny?

KENNY. Lemme finish before you talk business. You talk business while you eat it makes you sick. Remember that.

DOUG. I was just going to say that I thought you finished so I put my cigarette out in your linguini.

(KENNY sees the cigarette.)

KENNY. You are really fucked, Doug.

DOUG. I understand what you're saying. My feeling was that since you didn't care for the linguini—

KENNY. I mean are you an animal, or what? That is just the kind of thing a fucking animal would do, put its cigarette out in somebody's dinner.

DOUG. Kenny, this name calling is the mark of a lunatic. I know in my heart that you are far better than that—

KENNY. I come in here and you bullshit me and you set me up with your happily married waitress and now you put out your cigarettes in my food. Tell me what you want.

DOUG. I want to be partners, Kenny, plain and simple. Your people put up the money and Gary and me will make this place go. I absolutely guarantee it.

KENNY. How come it's not going now? And don't talk to me about jellyfish.

DOUG. Well, it takes time to get established in this business. The previous owners were clinically insane . . .

KENNY. The place was packed when they owned it —

DOUG. It was a dump, a dive— 'member when we looked in here, Gary?

GARY. It was a real dump, just like Doug is saying.

KENNY. Packed, every night. Then you and your brother come in with your magic touch and the place is a graveyard. You tell me why my people should buy in.

DOUG. It's an investment in the future. It's an investment in people like me and Gary that you respect.

KENNY. (*Opening his briefcase.*) Let's get one thing straight. I don't respect you. I look at the figures you did for the summer—

DOUG. Forget the figures—

GARY. It takes time to build it up—

KENNY. You did what, two thousand a week—

DOUG. Something like that—

KENNY You don't know? And you're in charge?

DOUG. Approximately that, yes.

GARY. Actually, it was fifteen hundred, Doug.

DOUG. Gary, would you let me handle this?

GARY. (*Opening his briefcase.*) Doug, I got the figures right here, from April when we opened up—

KENNY. I think it's two thousand, Gary—

DOUG. What difference does it make? What are we talking about?

KENNY. We're talking about the money you took in before you paid your bills. My people get very excited by money.

DOUG. Gary! Would you leave the business to me? That is an order from the very top of the organization!

GARY. It's okay, Doug, they're right here—

(*DOUG turns on KENNY, who also has taken papers from his briefcase.*)

DOUG. Put the papers away, Kenny. We should be

talking man to man like men—

KENNY. (*Looking at his papers.*) Yeah, two thousand.

GARY. How come I only show fifteen hundred?

KENNY. These are the figures you gave me, Doug.

DOUG. It's small change, whatever it is. I think we got more important things to discuss here than a few dollars—

KENNY. Lemme see that, Gary. (*KENNY compares the papers.*) Gary? We got two sets of figures here, you know that?

GARY. These are the only ones I ever saw.

(KENNY starts packing up his briefcase.)

DOUG. This makes me very sad. A family friend, a man I have counted on for over fifteen years. A man who unfortunately has a serious problem with the sauce. Let the record show that I have stood by the man right up until this very moment. Gary, it is time for me to lower the boom on our bookkeeper.

(KENNY stands up.)

DOUG. What, you got a date, Kenny? Must be pretty important to leave in the middle of a business meeting.

KENNY. You been skimming off the top, Doug, haven't you?

DOUG. Kenny, I am embarrassed for your sake that you would even think something like that. I will not dignify it with words.

KENNY. You're either lying to him or lying to me. Which is it?

DOUG. I'm not lying to anybody.

KENNY. (*Puts his card on table.*) When you guys declare bankruptcy, you're gonna need a good lawyer. Just so you don't get screwed again, Gary. (*KENNY starts for the door.*)

DOUG. Would you listen to reason, Kenny? You and me should be working together, I'm telling you, we're soul mates—

(*KENNY exits.*)

DOUG. Fucking hood. I was all set to throw him out on his ass anyway. He knew it, too, that's why he left. Fucking chicken-shit.

GARY. What's the story, Doug? I trusted you with the books.

LUCY. (*Enters from the kitchen.*) What happened to the sure thing?

GARY. He left.

LUCY. So we pull out. Doug, write us that check, would you?

GARY. You don't understand. It's too late. We gotta go bankrupt. We needed a bail-out and Kenny's all we could find.

LUCY. How much did you lose, Gary?

GARY. I put everything in.

LUCY. No you didn't. Everything? How come you didn't tell me that, Gary?

GARY. This was my thing. I always wanted to be partners with Doug.

DOUG. Gary's right. You gotta take some risks if you're ever gonna make a big hit.

GARY. We came close. We just ran outta time.

DOUG. Exactly. I'd say it was one hundred percent successful in every way except money—

LUCY. You got it all figured out, right? Now you can figure out how to clean up. (*SHE takes off her apron.*)

DOUG. That's not my side of the business.

LUCY. Me and Gary have been cleaning up this joint all summer. Now it's your turn.

DOUG. When the chips are down you really find out what people are made of, don't you? I thought you were a team player, Lucy.

LUCY. What are you saying?

DOUG. I'm not saying anything. You were with Kenny in the kitchen. Then he bailed out of the deal. That's all I'm saying.

LUCY. Let's go, Gary. It's getting late.

GARY. (*Staring at Doug.*) Me and Doug got some business to settle.

LUCY. What kind of business?

GARY. It's between him and me.

LUCY. I'm part of this, too, Gary.

GARY. I'll be home real soon.

LUCY. I won't be there.

GARY. Where you gonna be?

LUCY. Someplace else. Don't bother waiting up, Gary. (*LUCY exits.*)

GARY. Lucy!

DOUG. Women don't understand business, even the smart ones. I don't know what it is.

GARY. Tell me about the money, Doug.

DOUG. Gary, you gotta look into your own mental mind and decide something. You gotta decide if you're gonna trust your brother who you know your whole life or some lying, whoring, two-bit mob lackey who comes in here and drinks our booze and eats our food and sticks us with the tab. Which is it?

GARY. You must have changed somebody's figures.

DOUG. Yes, and that is standard business practice in this kind of situation, as you should well know. I changed the figures around so the man would come in with us. I did that out of love and respect for you and your tragic financial situation. And it makes me very fucking sad that you would think otherwise, Gary. If you still don't trust me, then come by my apartment tomorrow. I will take you through the books and you will see that I am an honest man who was trying to cheat Kenny, not you, my only brother.

GARY. I just want to be sure, I mean I got Lucy and the kid and the car.

DOUG. You impress me, Gary. You have showed me a lot of guts and determination.

GARY. Really?

DOUG. What I am saying is that I am willing to give you another chance as my partner in a venture that makes this restaurant look like the pathetic bullshit we both knew it to be from the start.

GARY. I always liked this place. You did, too. That's why we bought it.

DOUG. Don't insult our intelligence. You and I were put on this earth for better things than slinging hash for drunken teenagers. Right?

GARY. Yeah, right.

DOUG. Then welcome aboard.

GARY. To what?

DOUG. To a new venture, which frankly is too big

even to talk about among people. (*DOUG starts for the door.*) I gotta make some phone calls. Get Kenny in to unload this dump.

GARY. I thought you hated Kenny.

DOUG. True, I hate him. But I respect him, and he will represent us as we move into the bankruptcy phase of our business.

GARY. We can't leave Mike in there.

DOUG. These calls are just a little more important than cleaning up. Let me take care of everything. As my brother, I think you owe me that at the very least, after what has happened here tonight. I trust you have learned your lesson.

GARY. What lesson?

DOUG. Think about it, Gary. Think about it while you are cleaning up tonight. I learn a lesson from every business deal, and that is one of the keys to my own personal success. Do you wanna be a success or not? That's the question you have to look in the mirror and ask yourself.

GARY. Yeah, I wanna be a success.

(*DOUG exits.*)

GARY. Hey, Mike? You okay?

BLACKOUT

Scene 2

(Classical MUSIC and the BACKGROUND SOUNDS of a crowded restaurant. A recorded voice saying "Wilson, party of twelve, your table is ready." Then LIGHTS up on Kenny's Place, formerly the Beachside Bar and Grill. GARY and DOUG are standing by the door, casually dressed. ERICA, a very young waitress, approaches them.)

ERICA. Thanks for your patience. My name is Erica and I want to thank you for coming to Kenny's Place. We should have a table for you in just a minute.

GARY. Is it always this crowded?

ERICA. Oh, it's been a madhouse ever since we opened up. Especially on weekends.

GARY. We didn't think we'd need a reservation. It didn't used to be like this—

ERICA. I know what you mean, I came in here once just to use the phone. What a dump!

DOUG. Yeah, but hey, it's the same place, same location.

GARY. I wonder why no one ever came in before?

ERICA. From what I hear it was just bad management, they ran it right into the ground. Oh, I almost forgot, we require jackets in the dining room.

DOUG. Jackets in the dining room?

ERICA. The manager thinks that if people look nice then they act nice.

GARY. Let's get outta here, Doug. This was a bad idea—

DOUG. Gary, this is a man we trusted, a man we hired to represent us during bankruptcy. He double-billed us, he did shoddy work, then he stole our place. Now I can't even get him on the telephone.

GARY. What I am saying, is, I don't want to mess with Kenny's people.

DOUG. Kenny does not scare me and his people do not scare me. What I want to do is tell the dirty son of a bitch exactly what I think of him and then I wanna break every fucking bone in his body. We will walk out of here tonight with a settlement. I guarantee it.

ERICA. I'll get you jackets. (*ERICA exits.*)

DOUG. Can you believe this? Dinner jackets?

(ERICA returns with white jackets for them. GARY and DOUG put on the jackets, which are far too big. SHE leads them to a very bad table.)

ERICA. Can I get you something from the bar?

DOUG. Jack on the rocks. Make it a double.

GARY. Something with no alcohol—

ERICA. How's Perrier with a twist?

GARY. Yeah, fine.

ERICA. Our specials are on the board.

(KENNY comes over. HE's been making his way from table to table glad-handing people.)

KENNY. Doug! Gary! Great to see you again!

DOUG. You trying to make fools out of us, or what?

KENNY. Nah, I figure you can do that all by yourself, Doug.

DOUG. You fucked us over, Kenny.

KENNY. I got you a table as soon as I saw you waiting.

DOUG. That isn't the problem. I know in my heart that

you didn't intend to stab us in the back like you did. I am like you, Kenny, a guy who does business in good faith and cares about his fellow man. Because life is too short.

(ERICA brings the drinks. Before Doug can get his drink, KENNY turns to her.)

KENNY. Erica, doll? It's on the house for my friends, okay? And take those drinks back. I want them to have the Shipwreck.

ERICA. Sure, Mr. DeFries. (*ERICA exits.*)

DOUG. Listen to me, Kenny, because my train of thought is very important to me right now. I am a man who is standing on his feet. But Gary is in trouble. He doesn't understand why his own attorney would steal the family business, shove him into the gutter, kick him in the face, then charge him twice for it. I have told him that it is a misunderstanding that can be dealt with issue by issue so that all parties are in agreement. We'll start with the double-billing, then move on the death threats and you stealing our business.

KENNY. You guys get a chance to look at the menu?

DOUG. I wish you would communicate with me, Kenny.

KENNY. I am communicating, Doug. I am asking what you think of the menu and I am waiting for an answer. If that isn't communicating then I don't know what is. What do you think of Michael's menu?

GARY. Michael?

KENNY. Sure, Michael.

GARY. Our Mike?

KENNY. It turns out he's got a real talent for nouvelle

cuisine.

DOUG. The last time I saw Mike he was crawling through his own vomit with a belt tied around his arm.

KENNY. Michael has come a long way. I got him into rehab, and it's really given a boost to his self-esteem. See, Michael needs a lot of structure, a lot of encouragement, and, for lack of a better word, Michael needs love.

GARY. I remember days when Mike was unable to locate the kitchen.

KENNY. When you get to know Michael, I mean really know him, you find out that he is a very sensitive, spiritual kind of guy. And let's face it, the man can cook.

(ERICA brings two Shipwrecks. They are enormous rum drinks with lots of fruit and a plastic ship on top.)

KENNY. You need a hook for a place like this. We hit on the Shipwreck. Tell me what you think.

DOUG. Kenny, I am not trying to be ungrateful, but the fact is, I want a straight shot of honest booze.

(ERICA exits.)

KENNY. I already got an offer for four times what I paid. I could unload it and clean up.

DOUG. I'm starting to get mad, Kenny.

GARY. Kenny? I gotta ask you. How did you do it? I mean how did you get this crowd?

KENNY. You guys, you were catering to problem drinkers, drifters, hookers, kids who got thrown out of their homes, third-rate pimps. Your kind of people, but none of 'em with an extra buck to spend. Me, I went after recreational drug-users, young professionals, you know the type. People smart enough to make money but too dumb to know what to do with it.

DOUG. The fact is, the minute the ink was dry on the papers the jellyfish cleared out, and that's the only reason you got a crowd. Me and my brother were deceived and sold down the river by you, and we have come here tonight to see that justice is done.

(LUCY approaches the table. She is wearing a very sexy waitress outfit.)

LUCY. Gary! What are you doing here?

GARY. We're doing business.

LUCY. Kenny wanted to keep me on. It's a little different than before.

GARY. Sure looks it.

LUCY. Are you okay, Gary?

GARY. Yeah, terrific. Fine. I'm okay. You know . . .

LUCY. Where you been?

GARY. Out of town. The new business. Before it went under.

LUCY. It's really good to see you.

GARY. Yeah, you too. So things are okay?

LUCY. Yeah, pretty much okay. Overall. Hi, Doug.

DOUG. Hi, Lucy.

LUCY. *(To Gary.)* So . . . did she tell you the specials?

KENNY. What's the story with you two?

LUCY. We're married.

KENNY. You and Gary are married? To each other?

LUCY. Yeah, to each other.

KENNY. How long have you been married?

GARY. What is it, six years?

LUCY. Right, eight years.

KENNY. How come nobody told me this?

LUCY. We've been . . . living apart lately.

GARY. Separated.

LUCY. Yeah, we been separated.

KENNY. I'll be goddamned. Well, congratulations.

GARY. For what?

KENNY. You know. Being married. I feel like you're newlyweds 'cause I just found out. I feel like we oughta have champagne.

LUCY. I guess I should be taking your order or something.

KENNY. Sit down, would you?

(LUCY sits.)

KENNY. How long have you two been separated?

LUCY. Ever since we lost the restaurant. Gary needed time to get his head together, wasn't that it?

GARY. I was all over the place. Money problems, you name it.

KENNY. So how are you doing, Gary? I mean, is your head together again, or what?

GARY. Pretty together, yeah. As much as it ever is. So how's Tommy?

LUCY. He's okay. He misses you, Gary.

DOUG. Fuck this shit. I'm gonna look around the place. *(DOUG exits.)*

KENNY. You didn't tell me you two were married. She finally tells me she's married, but she didn't mention you. And that was only after I chased her around the kitchen a coupla times.

GARY. We needed a partner real bad.

KENNY. And Lucy was the bait?

GARY. Actually, Doug was pushing that particular plan.

KENNY. That brother of yours. He's a nasty piece of work. (*Calls out.*) Erica!

ERICA. (*Comes to the table.*) Yes, Mr. DeFries?

KENNY. You know the other guy in this party?

ERICA. The guy with the big coat?

KENNY. Keep him busy for a while. I want to talk to my friends. Take him to the bar upstairs. Tell him nobody understands you. Talk about your childhood. When we're done down here, we'll have him thrown out on his ass, okay?

ERICA. Very good, Mr. DeFries.

DOUG. (*Comes back to the table.*) I give this place six months, Kenny. Tops. You can't even get a real drink.

ERICA. I'm sorry you had a problem, sir. May I suggest the upstairs lounge? I think you'll like it. It's very . . . cozy.

DOUG. (*Sizing her up.*) You ain't off the hook, Kenny.

ERICA. This way, please.

(*ERICA leads DOUG off.*)

KENNY. You like the Shipwreck, Gary?

GARY. It's kinda hard to drink—

KENNY. It's impossible to drink. Nobody drinks 'em. They cost twelve bucks and we use the same ones over and over. It's a cutthroat business whenever the public is involved. So what are we gonna do with the two of you?

LUCY. I guess that's something me and Gary will have to work out sometime.

KENNY. Let's get off your problems for just a minute and talk about me. I picked this place up out of the pure meanness in my heart. And out of cold-blooded revenge I built it into what you see before you tonight. I'm thinking you two could maybe manage the place for me. You got the experience, you're honest . . . and since I robbed the place from you to begin with, I give you back half ownership.

GARY. Me and Doug?

KENNY. You and Lucy. If I hear you ever cut him in then I'll put this place under. I'll have it knocked down and torched and I'll personally dump the ashes in the ocean. Then I'll have all your knuckles broken so you'll remember not to do such a stupid-ass thing ever again.

GARY. You sound pretty definite about Doug's involvement.

KENNY. That's the deal. I been through two night managers already. I want somebody I can trust.

GARY. Lucy? What do you think?

LUCY. I never wanted to split up in the first place, Gary.

GARY. Neither did I. I guess we had to.

LUCY. For a while. We don't need to stay split up as long as your head is pretty much together again.

GARY. It's getting together real quick seeing you, Lucy.

KENNY. There, that wasn't so hard, was it?

GARY. Thanks, Kenny.

KENNY. Don't thank me—it's a perfect deal. I get a chance to really fuck somebody over and do a good deed all at once. How often does that happen?

ERICA. (*Enters.*) He's not one for conversation.

(*DOUG comes over to the table.*)

KENNY. How'd you like the view, Doug?

DOUG. You can't do anything about the fog?

KENNY. My people will be glad to look into it. Hell, it worked with the jellyfish.

DOUG. (*Sitting down.*) Here's our plan, Kenny, and you can tell it to these goddam people of yours. Me and Gary want a piece of your weekly action for the next year to make up for what you done.

KENNY. That's a helluva plan, Doug. You come up with that all by yourself?

DOUG. I am not one to make threats, Kenny, but if you don't go along with that, then I will go to the proper authorities and have you disbarred. Because you failed to honestly represent our interests.

KENNY. I would say I went far beyond that, Doug. As your attorney, I'd advise you that my behavior was out and out criminal.

DOUG. I'll have to take your word for your dishonesty. When me and Gary go public with how we have been treated, your reputation will be destroyed.

KENNY. Doug, you should understand by now that my reputation rests on my association with organized crime and my contempt for both due legal process and even the barest essentials of human decency. That's why people come to me. So anything you could allege about my dishonorable conduct would only help my reputation and bring me new clients.

DOUG. You admit to cheating us. That is the framework of our discussion. Now we must talk percentages. What are you willing to give us as an initial offer?

KENNY. Tell him, Gary.

GARY. You don't need to do anything for me, Doug. I can take care of myself.

DOUG. Let me handle this, Gary. Every time you open your mouth it is another giant step backwards.

KENNY. Gary already got what he wants, right, Gary?

GARY. Kenny made us managers.

DOUG. What are you talking about?

KENNY. Half owners, too.

DOUG. Gary, you cut the deal without me?

GARY. That's right.

DOUG. What'd you have to give up?

KENNY. Nothing. Gary played hardball.

GARY. Me and Kenny worked it out man to man, like men.

DOUG. I'll be goddamned! This is true, Kenny?

KENNY. Fifty percent owners.

DOUG. You've been learning quite a lot from watching me in action. I guess all we got to do is get it down on paper—

GARY. This don't include you, Doug.

DOUG. You said he made us fifty percent owners.

GARY. Us. Me and Lucy.

DOUG. I don't get it.

LUCY. It's real simple, Doug. You're out.

DOUG. We talk later, right, Gary?

GARY. There's nothing to talk about.

DOUG. But you bring me in at a future date—

KENNY. You will never be a part of this operation, Doug.

LUCY. You said you were cutting this deal for Gary. Gary's taken care of himself pretty good.

DOUG. You can't do that to me. I got us the place to begin with. I brought Kenny in. I got us all together. You can't be cutting deals without me, because I am the key figure. For Christ's sake I even drove you here tonight.

GARY. Lucy will drive me home.

DOUG. You are all going to regret this savage attack on me. Kenny, there's nothing to stop me from going to the authorities—

KENNY. That would be an unwise course of action in terms of your physical well-being.

DOUG. Gary, if you do not beg me to stay and make me an equal partner then I disown you as my brother. (*Beat.*) That is to say you are ineligible for future ventures that could make us both rich. (*Beat.*) On holidays I will refuse to come to your house and join the other members of our family whom I detest, as you well know. I will punish every one of you by staying alone in my apartment.

LUCY. We oughta get this in writing.

DOUG. Gary, I am speaking to you as your brother. Not as your business partner, not as the loyal friend I have been to you, not as your mentor, your guiding light through the formative years, not as the inspiration I know I have provided to you in your countless hours of blackest despair. No, I am speaking to you as your only brother for all eternity, and what I am saying to you is for God sakes, please make me a partner in this restaurant.

GARY. I can't do it, Doug. And I don't want to do it. This is my gig. Now sit down because you're bothering our customers.

DOUG. What did you say to me?

GARY. I am not speaking to you as your brother, Doug. I am speaking to you as the manager of Kenny's Place. Get the hell out of here.

KENNY. Atta boy, Gary.

DOUG. Look at this. My own family is putting me out on the street with backing from the Mob. This is a deal that has truly gone bad.

KENNY. Hang in there, Dougie. There's always room for a guy with brass balls.

DOUG. You mean it, Kenny? Because if that is true, I will call you on the telephone. I am an idea-man.

KENNY. An idea-man with brass balls. That's even better. I look forward to hearing from you, Doug. (*KENNY exits.*)

DOUG. I am giving you one last chance to come to your senses, Gary.

GARY. C'mon, Doug.

DOUG. You know, I've decided something, Gary. I've decided to leave.

LUCY. That's a real good decision, Doug.

DOUG. You still don't see what has happened, Gary. You don't see that Kenny and me are now like this. He has welcomed me into his organization. I am one of Kenny's people, and you are left behind, like always. The night manager of a cave. The captain of a sinking ship. That is you and this is me. (*DOUG goes to the exit.*)

GARY. Doug?

DOUG. What is it, Gary?

GARY. Could you leave the coat on your way out? (*Beat.*) It don't fit anyway.

(DOUG takes off the white jacket and exits. GARY and LUCY are sitting at the table.)

BLACKOUT

THE END

COSTUME PLOT

GARY
a cheap suit
a casual shirt or tee-shirt
pants
an oversized sports jacket

DOUG
jeans
Hawaiian shirt
a casual shirt
an oversized sports jacket

LUCY
a simple waitress outfit with apron
a sexy, stylish waitress outfit

KENNY
a suit that means business

ERICA
a sexy waitress outfit

PROPERTY PLOT

a glass of milk

two briefcases

various drinks (Jack Daniels, scotch)

a checkbook

a plate of linguini

cigarettes and lighter

two sets of papers

a business card

a glass of Perrier

two "Shipwrecks" (enormous "theme" drinks)

Other Publications for Your Interest

OTHER PEOPLE'S MONEY
(LITTLE THEATRE—DRAMA)

By JERRY STERNER

3 men, 2 women—One Set

Wall Street takeover artist Lawrence Garfinkle's intrepid computer is going "tilt" over the undervalued stock of New England Wire & Cable. He goes after the vulnerable company, buying up its stock to try and take over the company at the annual meeting. If the stockholders back Garfinkle, they will make a bundle—but what of the 1200 employees? What of the local community? Too bad, says Garfinkle, who would then liquidate the company—take the money and run. Set against the charmingly rapacious financier are Jorgenson, who has run the company since the Year One and his chief operations officer, Coles, who understands, unlike the genial Jorgenson, what a threat Garfinkle poses to the firm. They bring in Kate, a bright young woman lawyer, who specializes in fending off takeovers—and who is the daughter of Jorgenson's administrative assistant, Bea. Kate must not only contend with Garfinkle—she must also move Jorgenson into taking decisive action. Should they use "greenmail"? Try to find a "White Knight"? Employ a "shark repellent"? This compelling drama about Main Street vs. Wall Street is as topical and fresh as today's headlines, giving its audience an inside look at what's *really going on* in this country and asking trenchant questions, not the least of which is whether a corporate raider is really the creature from the Black Lagoon of capitalism or the Ultimate Realist come to save business from itself.

(#17064)

THE DOWNSIDE
(LITTLE THEATRE—COMEDY)

By RICHARD DRESSER

6 men, 2 women—Combination Interior

These days, American business is a prime target for satire, and no recent play has cut as deep, with more hilarious results, than this superb new comedy from the Long Wharf Theatre, Mark & Maxwell, a New Jersey pharmaceuticals firm, has acquired U.S. rights to market an anti-stress drug manufactured in Europe, pending F.D.A. approval; but the marketing executives have got to come up with a snazzy ad campaign by January—and here we are in December! The irony is that nowhere is this drug more needed than right there at Mark & Maxwell, a textbook example of corporate ineptitude, where it seems all you have to do to get ahead is look good in a suit. The marketing strategy meetings get more and more pointless and frenetic as the deadline approaches. These meetings are "chaired" by Dave, the boss, who is never actually there—he is a voice coming out of a box, as Dave phones in while jetting to one meeting or another, eventually directing the ad campaign on his mobile phone while his plane is being hijacked! Doesn't matter to Dave, though—what matters is the possible "downside" of this new drug: hallucinations. "Ridiculous", says the senior marketing executive Alan: who then proceeds to tell how Richard Nixon comes to his house in the middle of the night to visit..."Richard Dresser's deft satirical sword pinks the corporate image repeatedly, leaving the audience amused but thoughtful."—Meriden Record. "Funny and ruthlessly cynical."—Phila. Inquirer. "A new comedy that is sheer delight."—Westport News. "The Long Wharf audience laughed a lot, particularly those with office training. But they were also given something to ponder about the way we get things done in America these days, or rather pretend to get things done. No wonder the Japanese are winning."—L.A. Times.

(#6718)

ALONE AT THE BEACH
(LITTLE THEATRE—COMEDY)
By RICHARD DRESSER

4 men, 3 women—Combination Interior/Exterior

"So you thought the kind of comedy that sends audiences home happy had disappeared from the American theatre scene? *"Wrong!"* enthused the Louisville Courier-Journal over this literate, witty comedy, which had the audience at Actors Theatre of Louisville's famed Humana Festival whooping with laughter. George, a mild-mannered man in his mid-30's, has inherited a beach house in the Hamptons on Long Island. In order to afford to keep it, he has let out rooms to boarders, Manhattan-ites desparate to get out of the city on weekends. Blindly, and blithely, George has not actually *met* any of these denizens of the yuppie sector of the urban jungle. If everyone were Great Fun and Easy To Get Along With, everyone would have a great time—but the audience, of course, wouldn't. Who wants to watch a bunch of friendly, well-adjusted people have Fun In The Sun? Thankfully, Dresser gives us a motley crew of urban neurotics, male and female, who begin to drive George, and everyone else, crazy the moment they arrive. Somehow, though, everyone survives the experience, egos intact; and, in fact, some of the most unlikely romances develop, before everyone has to face reality: Labor Day and, subsequently, the trek back to New York City for good—until next summer? "Has a unique sparkle." New Albany Tribune. "A winner...a riotously funny sex farce."—Detroit News. "A charming romp that should turn up in regional and community theatres all over the place."—Houston Post. "Has the pacing of a Neil Simon script but with some of the dry, more cerebral wit of Jules Feiffer."—Evansville Courier.

(#3118)

EMILY
(ADVANCED GROUPS—SERIOUS COMEDY)
By STEPHEN METCALFE

8 men, 4 women, to play a variety of roles.
Bare stage, w/drops, wings, projections & wagons; or, may be unit set.

This brilliant, cynical, contemporary new comedy by the author of *Strange Snow, Vikings, Sorrows and Sons* and *The Incredibly Famous Willy Rivers* dares to take what amounts to a politically "incorrect" stance about the successful "New Woman." Emily is a successful New York City stockbroker who mixes it up with the boys and always comes out on top. In fact, she was described by one misguided critic as coming off like a "man in drag"; because, as we all know, women are caring, loving, nurturing creatures—and what a wonderful world it would be if *they* were in positions of political and/or business power, instead of those insensitive jerks, the *men*. Emily is just as cynical and ruthless as any man in her position; until, that is, she meets a caring, sensitive, aspiring actor (in other words, a nice guy with no money) who doesn't fall for her manipulative ruses; but, rather, for the real Emily he sees inside the ruthless yuppie—who may, or may not, exist. "Glorious...a sparkling comedy with bite to it. The title character is a gold mine of a role for an actress."—San Diego Tribune. "A real winner...a bravura balancing act right on the edge of sentimentality, finally and triumphantly crystalline in its emotional honesty...A triumph."—San Diego Union.

(#7076)